Awww...

take a sweet moment with God

Devotions
inspired by
awesome,
amazing
animals of
the wild

Inspired
by Faith

Awww...take a sweet moment with God
ISBN 978-0-9914172-2-3

Published by Product Concept Mfg., Inc.
2175 N. Academy Circle #200, Colorado Springs, CO 80909

©2014 Product Concept Mfg., Inc. All rights reserved.

Written and Compiled by Vicki J. Kuyper
in association with Product Concept Mfg., Inc.

All scripture quotations are from the King James version
of the Bible unless otherwise noted.

Scriptures taken from the Holy Bible,
New International Version®, NIV®.
Copyright © 1973, 1978, 1984 by Biblica, Inc.™
Used by permission of Zondervan.
All rights reserved worldwide.
www.zondervan.com

Sayings not having a credit listed are contributed by writers
for Product Concept Mfg., Inc. or in a rare case,
the author is unknown.

Awww...
take a sweet moment with God

Devotions
inspired by
awesome,
amazing
animals of
the wild

The worst sin towards our fellow creatures is
not to hate them, but to be indifferent to them.
That's the essence of inhumanity.

George Bernard Shaw

Our world is filled with amazing animals. From hummingbirds to humpbacks, the more we learn about them, the more in awe we find we'll be of the One who created them. Add some "awe" to your day! Get to know God, and His world, a little better...one sweet moment at a time.

THE SPEEDY CHEETAH

A Lamborghini Gallardo sports car can reach 60 miles per hour in 3.2 seconds. A cheetah can match that speed in 3 seconds flat. But that isn't even a cheetah's top speed. These amazing cats have been clocked at 71 mph. That makes the cheetah the fastest animal on earth. (Some birds fly faster than the cheetah can run, but then they aren't technically "on earth," right?)

Cheetahs need God's gift of speed because their light body weight and blunt claws don't offer much protection. They also have poor night vision, can't climb trees or roar. So they run. Fast. But they can't keep up their maximum speed for more than a few minutes. This is why cheetahs reserve their super speed sprints for escaping a predator or picking up a "fast food" meal. Most of their life is spent at a much more leisurely pace.

The Need for Speed

The cheetah has the ability to exceed the speed limit on most highways. But it can't keep that pace for long. It tires quickly. And so do we.

God created us with a cheetah-like ability to move at top speed—when the situation calls for it. We can multi-task our way through the holidays, run across the street before WALK turns to DON'T WALK, clock some overtime to meet a deadline and deprive ourselves of sleep to meet the needs of a newborn. For short periods of time. Then, like the cheetah, we need to slow back down to a more sustainable, God-designed pace.

When we schedule breathing room into our day, enjoy vacations with those we love or take an afternoon nap on a lazy Sunday afternoon, we're taking good care of the body God has given us. Then, when life speeds up again, we'll have enough energy in reserve to pick up the pace when needed.

There is more to life than increasing its speed.
Mahatma Gandhi

MOST MEN PURSUE PLEASURE WITH SUCH
BREATHLESS HASTE THAT THEY HURRY PAST IT.
SØREN KIERKEGAARD

They that wait upon the Lord shall renew
their strength; they shall mount up with wings
as eagles; they shall run, and not be weary;
and they shall walk, and not faint.
Isaiah 40:31

HE WHO SEWS HURRY REAPS INDIGESTION.
ROBERT LOUIS STEVENSON

Never be in a hurry;
do everything quietly and in a calm spirit.
Do not lose your inner peace for anything
whatsoever, even if your whole
world seems upset.
Francis de Sales

BE STILL, AND KNOW THAT I AM GOD.
PSALM 46:10

A first-rate organizer is never in a hurry.
He is never late. He always keeps up his sleeve
a margin for the unexpected.
Arnold Bennett

ADOPT THE PACE OF NATURE:
HER SECRET IS PATIENCE.
HENRY DAVID THOREAU

POLAR BEAR COUTURE

Polar bears wear God-given camouflage. Though their fur looks white or yellow, it's actually pigment-free. Each hollow strand is similar to the surrounding snow in that it's transparent and reflects light. This helps keep a polar bear warm. Since polar bears don't hibernate, they need all the protection they can get from the elements. In their Arctic home, temperatures can range from −40° to −90° Fahrenheit during the winter.

But the polar bears' fur does more than help keep them warm. It also helps them blend in with their icy habitat. This makes them formidable predators. If it weren't for their black noses, they'd be almost indistinguishable from their surroundings. However, on a clear day a polar bear's nose can be spotted through binoculars from 6 miles away.

Similar, but Not the Same

For years, it was believed that polar bears would occasionally hide their black noses behind their paws when hunting seals to help better conceal themselves from their prey. Recently, researchers put this rumor to rest through months of first-hand observation. They concluded this "rumor" was passed along because it was something we humans might do if put in the polar bear's situation.

At times, we view God the way we once viewed polar bears: We expect Him to act the same way we do. But it's us who were created in God's image, not the other way around. We reflect some of God's characteristics, but we are not a mirror-perfect reflection of Him. His wisdom, power and perspective are so far above our own that our minds cannot fully understand them. That's where faith comes in.

Choosing to place our trust in Someone we don't fully understand sounds a bit daunting. But the more time we spend getting to know God, and the closer we're drawn into His love, the easier it becomes to trust Him. Even when (from our limited point of view) life doesn't always make sense.

Many other signs truly did Jesus
in the presence of his disciples, which are not
written in this book: But these are written, that
ye might believe that Jesus is the Christ,
the Son of God; and that believing ye
might have life through his name.
John 20:30-31

READ THE SCRIPTURE,
NOT ONLY AS A HISTORY, BUT AS A LOVE-LETTER
SENT TO YOU FROM GOD.
THOMAS WATSON

Jesus wept.
John 11:35

THE BIBLE IS A LETTER GOD HAS SENT TO US;
PRAYER IS A LETTER WE SEND TO HIM.
MATTHEW HENRY

In our fluctuations of feeling, it is well
to remember that Jesus admits no change
in his affections; your heart is not the
compass Jesus saileth by.
Samuel Rutherford

ALL I HAVE SEEN TEACHES ME TO TRUST THE
CREATOR FOR ALL I HAVE NOT SEEN.
RALPH WALDO EMERSON

Jesus did many other things as well.
If every one of them were written down,
I suppose that even the whole world would not
have room for the books that would be written.
John 21:25 NIV

I LOVE TO THINK OF NATURE
AS AN UNLIMITED BROADCASTING STATION
THROUGH WHICH GOD SPEAKS TO US EVERY
HOUR, IF WE WILL ONLY TUNE IN.
GEORGE WASHINGTON CARVER

What Elephants Never Forget

One of nature's most closely-knit social groups is an elephant herd. Another name for this group is a memory. That's because the group's survival is dependent on the incredible memory of its eldest matriarch. She remembers the location of distant watering holes and can differentiate between "known" elephants and those she's never met who may pose a threat.

With the exception of whales, elephants' super-sized 11 pound brains have more complex folds than any other animals'. This is believed to indicate intelligence. But elephants are not just smart. They're also emotionally sensitive. Research has documented evidence of elephant altruism, humor, joy and grief.

Elephants care for their sick, comfort distraught "children" and even bury their dead with sticks and leaves, then remain by the grave for several hours. They've been known to revisit the bones of a deceased family member and run their trunks along the teeth of its lower jaw-bone. This is the same way they greet an elephant "friend" when it's alive.

Putting Our Memory to Work

It's easy to remember deeply emotional experiences...the joys we treasure, the hardships we've endured, the victories we've celebrated, the wounds we're still waiting to heal. We may even spend time revisiting these in our minds, for better or for worse.

But the joys and sorrows of others come to mind, and heart, much less readily. That's because it takes effort to remember something that hasn't happened to us personally. But remembering, and empathizing, with those in our "herd" of friends, family and even casual acquaintances is something God encourages us to do.

We've been created in God's own image, as emotional beings. And God's given us brains big enough and powerful enough to be able to reach out in compassion to offer love and comfort to those around us. If only we could remember to do it! That's where prayer comes in. Ask God to help you be more emotionally aware of those around you—and find ways to touch someone's life today in a positive way.

Nature's great masterpiece, an elephant;
the only harmless great thing.
John Donne

In making our decisions,
we must use the brains that God has given us.
But we must also use our hearts,
which He also gave us.
Fulton Oursler

Rejoice with them that do rejoice,
and weep with them that weep.
Romans 12:15

Kind hearts are the gardens;
Kind thoughts are the roots;
Kind words are the flowers;
Kind deeds are the fruits.
Henry Wadsworth Longfellow

God does not comfort us to make us comfortable, but to make us comforters.
John Henry Jowett

PRAISE BE TO THE GOD AND FATHER OF
OUR LORD JESUS CHRIST, THE FATHER OF
COMPASSION AND THE GOD OF ALL COMFORT,
WHO COMFORTS US IN ALL OUR TROUBLES,
SO THAT WE CAN COMFORT THOSE IN ANY
TROUBLE WITH THE COMFORT WE
OURSELVES RECEIVE FROM GOD.
2 CORINTHIANS 1:3—4 NIV

To ease another's heartache
is to forget one's own.
Abraham Lincoln

ANY GLIMPSE INTO THE LIFE OF AN
ANIMAL QUICKENS OUR OWN AND MAKES IT SO
MUCH THE LARGER AND BETTER IN EVERY WAY.
JOHN MUIR

Eye Spy

Magpies are clever birds. When something shiny catches their eye, they'll try their best to snatch it for their nest. Heaven forbid you momentarily remove a piece of jewelry when they're around.

But magpies have eyes for more than bling. They're also one of very few animals (including bottlenose dolphins, Asian elephants and several types of apes) that can recognize themselves in the mirror. When a small black sticker is placed on the black feathers of a magpie's neck, the bird has no reaction when faced with a mirror. But put a yellow sticker on its feathers and the bird will preen itself like a prom queen until that sticker is gone. This kind of self-recognition doesn't develop in humans until we're about 18 months old.

A KEY TO CONTENTMENT

There's a little bit of magpie in all of us. We pass a mirror and check ourselves out, making sure there's not a hair out of place—or a yellow sticker on our necks. If we don't like what we see, we primp and preen until we're satisfied with the results. And if something "shiny" catches our eye in a store window, we long to possess it. If we can afford it, we buy it. If we can't, we'll hold that image close in our thoughts, picturing how that special bauble will make our nest a better place, longing for the day we can make it our own.

Our eyes have a complicated relationship with our heart. Our satisfaction with life, and with ourselves, can be skewed by what we see in the mirror or an ad on TV—if we let it. Recognizing the presence of our inner-magpie is the first step toward reducing its power. The more we ignore its self-focused squawking, the more contented we'll find ourselves to be.

How things look on the outside of us depends on
how things are on the inside of us.
Henry Ward Beecher

I HAVE LEARNED TO BE CONTENT WHATEVER THE
CIRCUMSTANCES. I KNOW WHAT IT IS TO BE IN
NEED, AND I KNOW WHAT IT IS TO HAVE PLENTY.
I HAVE LEARNED THE SECRET OF
BEING CONTENT IN ANY AND EVERY SITUATION,
WHETHER WELL FED OR HUNGRY,
WHETHER LIVING IN PLENTY OR IN WANT.
PHILIPPIANS 4:11-12 NIV

He who is not contented with little
will never be satisfied with much.
Thomas Benton Brooks

WHERE YOUR TREASURE IS,
THERE WILL YOUR HEART BE ALSO.
MATTHEW 6:21

The discontented man finds no easy chair.
Benjamin Franklin

I AM ALWAYS CONTENT WITH THAT WHICH
HAPPENS, FOR I THINK THAT WHICH GOD
CHOOSES IS BETTER THAN WHAT I CHOOSE.
EPICTETUS

When we cannot find contentment in ourselves
it is useless to seek it elsewhere.
François de la Rochefoucauld

THE RAREST FEELING THAT EVER
LIGHTS A HUMAN FACE IS THE
CONTENTMENT OF A LOVING SOUL.
HENRY WARD BEECHER

A Little Work Horse

Shetland ponies are known for being cute, squat and shaggy—perfect for a petting zoo or a kiddie ride at the fair. But throughout history, the life of most Shetland ponies has been anything but frolic-filled.

The ponies' compact size and sturdy build make them perfect for hauling heavy loads, like peat soil and seaweed. They excelled at this job for centuries in their native home on the Shetland islands off the coast of Scotland. But in 1842, Great Britain passed a law prohibiting children from working in the coalmines. "Pit ponies" took over their jobs. Some of these ponies spent almost their entire lives underground.

In the late 1970s, this practice fell out of favor in the UK and the US. Today, many Shetlands have found a new calling—as "guide ponies" for the disabled. Though small in stature, Shetland ponies have proved over and over again that they're willing to work hard on our behalf.

Working Toward the Weekend

Work is more than just a way to pay the bills. It's an opportunity to use the gifts and abilities God has given us, to serve our community in a positive way, to learn how to follow and to lead. It's a proving ground for traits like discipline, patience, perseverance, sacrifice and humility. It's a way to honor God in a practical, down-to-earth setting.

God cares about our Mondays, our hump days and our late nights at the office just as much as He cares about our Sundays. If we're on the job, but our heart is somewhere else, we can't do our best. We'll be divided by distraction, instead of focused on the task at hand. And when we do less than our best, we won't experience a sense of pride and accomplishment in what we do. Instead, we'll begin to view our job as drudgery.

Every job matters. Whether we're performing heart surgery, driving a school bus or taking orders at a drive-thru, what we do makes a difference to God, to others and to ourselves. A job well done is essential to a life well lived.

Don't let yesterday use up too much of today.
Will Rogers

IT IS WORK WHICH GIVES FLAVOR TO LIFE.
HENRI-FRÉDÉRIC AMIEL

The work of today is the history of tomorrow,
and we are its makers.
Juliette Gordon Low

IF WE ALL DID THE THINGS
WE ARE REALLY CAPABLE OF DOING,
WE WOULD LITERALLY ASTOUND OURSELVES.
THOMAS EDISON

Far and away the best prize that life offers is the
chance to work hard at work worth doing.
Theodore Roosevelt

THE ARTIST IS NOTHING WITHOUT THE GIFT,
BUT THE GIFT IS NOTHING WITHOUT WORK.
EMILE ZOLA

Great works do not always lie in our way, but
every moment we may do little ones excellently,
that is, with great love.
Frances de Sales

WHATEVER YOU DO,
WORK AT IT WITH ALL YOUR HEART,
AS WORKING FOR THE LORD,
NOT FOR HUMAN MASTERS.
COLOSSIANS 3:23 NIV

THE ROLY-POLY HEDGEHOG

Whether they're exotic pets, ceramic figurines or embroidered on a cardigan sweater, hedgehogs are in! Male hedgehogs are called boars, females are sows and babies are known as hoglets. A group of hedgehogs? They're called "an array." But, regardless of what you call them, most people agree to call them "cute!"

A hedgehog's pointy nose, springy spines and waddling gait are all part of its appeal. But what seems to delight its fans most is the hedgehog's tendency to roll up in a ball when frightened. Predators can't "open" a hedgehog to get past its 5,000 quills to its more vulnerable face, eyes, limbs and tummy.

Though hedgehogs lead a mostly solitary life in the wild, they have been known to bond well with humans. Perhaps they realize what big fans we are.

THE VULNERABILITY OF LOVE

You don't have to be a hedgehog to feel vulnerable. We all long for the comfort of feeling safe. So, we roll ourselves up into a ball in countless ways throughout the day. We lock our doors, avert our eyes, give our full attention to our cell phones and social networks instead of to the people actually around us...

Yes, there's real danger in this world. But being vulnerable relationally isn't as dangerous as it is adventurous. Opening up to others does open us up to the possibility of being rejected or misunderstood. But, it's also the most reliable path toward being loved. And that's where our true longing lies. Feeling comfortable will never satisfy us like being on the receiving end of compassion.

Only when we're fully known can we be fully loved. That's why God's love is so different from that of anyone else we've ever met. He knows our deepest secrets, our most intimate longings, our greatest failures–every thought, word and deed. He sees us as we are and invites us into His loving embrace, a place where our vulnerability is cradled safely in His unconditional love.

There is only one happiness in life,
to love and be loved.
George Sand

THERE IS NO FEAR IN LOVE;
BUT PERFECT LOVE CASTETH OUT FEAR.
I JOHN 4:18

The greatest gift is a portion of thyself.
Ralph Waldo Emerson

I AM PERSUADED, THAT NEITHER DEATH,
NOR LIFE, NOR ANGELS, NOR PRINCIPALITIES,
NOR POWERS, NOR THINGS PRESENT,
NOR THINGS TO COME, NOR HEIGHT,
NOR DEPTH, NOR ANY OTHER CREATURE,
SHALL BE ABLE TO SEPARATE US
FROM THE LOVE OF GOD.
ROMANS 8:38-39

Behold, what manner of love the Father hath
bestowed upon us,
that we should be called the sons of God.
1 John 3:1

To love anyone is nothing else
than to wish that person good.
Thomas Aquinas

Love consists in this, that two solitudes protect
and touch and greet each other.
Rainer Maria Rilke

He who loves, trusts.
Proverb

BIRD BRAINED?

When it comes to size, the ostrich is a record breaker. It's the largest, and heaviest, of all birds. It also happens to be the fastest runner. Which is helpful, since it cannot fly. The ostrich also breaks the record for having the largest eyes of any land animal, measuring two inches in diameter. Despite having such enormous peepers, the ostrich has a tendency to run into things. Perhaps that's because its eye is larger than its brain. As a matter of fact, an ostrich brain would hardly fill a teaspoon. That doesn't bode well when it comes to making wise, complex decisions.

Maybe that's one reason why ostriches have been known to swallow just about anything, including rope, gloves, clocks, bicycle valves, jewelry...you name it. No nutritional value there. Of course, people have been known to devour diet soda and cream-filled cupcakes or try to break a record for consuming the most hot dogs. Birds of a feather, perhaps?

WISE MOVES

If you could be a bona-fide record breaker, what area would you want to excel in? Would it relate to your vocation? Creative endeavors? Physical prowess? Your financial bottom line? Your answer says a lot about what you treasure most.

In the book of 1 Kings in the Bible, God tells King Solomon to ask for anything he wants—and God says He will give it to him. Solomon doesn't ask to be the strongest, wealthiest, most powerful or best looking king around. Instead, he asks for the ability to discern wisely between good and evil so that he will be a good leader for his people. The whole kingdom benefited from Solomon's request.

Being wise isn't the same thing as being smart. Wisdom is using our intelligence and experience to make the most of our circumstances and abilities. It helps us discern what to do and say in any and every situation. So, stop, think and ask God for wisdom before moving forward with anything you consider important in your life. It's the wisest move you can make.

Wisdom is better than rubies;
and all things that may be desired
are not to be compared to it.
Proverbs 8:11

NO MAN WAS EVER WISE BY CHANCE.
SENECA

God gave Solomon wisdom and understanding
exceeding much, and largeness of heart,
even as the sand that is on the sea shore.
1 Kings 4:29

WISDOM IS THE RIGHT USE OF KNOWLEDGE.
CHARLES HADDON SPURGEON

The more accurately we search into the human mind, the stronger traces we everywhere find of the wisdom of him who made it.
Edmund Burke

IF ANY OF YOU LACK WISDOM, LET HIM ASK OF GOD, THAT GIVETH TO ALL MEN LIBERALLY.
JAMES 1:5

Who is the wise man?
He who learns from all men.
William Gladstone

HE THAT WALKETH WITH WISE MEN
SHALL BE WISE.
PROVERBS 13:20

Wisdom begins in wonder.
Socrates

THE FREE-SPIRITED GIRAFFE

Giraffes are a little like snowflakes. Each one bears a pattern of spots that's wholly unique. But that's not the only thing that's unique about giraffes. Their herds are a lot less structured than those of most other animals. Not only is it hard to tell who's the leader of the herd, individuals are free to wander off and join another herd at any time.

In this respect, giraffes are kind of free spirits. They lead relatively quiet lives, munching leaves, raising their young, and pretty much minding their own business when it comes to other animals. If they survive the first year of life, they're rarely in danger from predators. That's because giraffes can run 35 mph, step over a six-foot barrier and grow to be between 14 and 17 feet tall. It's little wonder the name giraffe comes from the Arabic word xirapha (zee-RAF-ah) or zarafah, that means "the one that walks very fast."

Breaking Away

There are times in our lives when it's best to follow in the footsteps of the giraffe, break away from the crowd and head off in a different direction. Although giraffes don't really exhibit courage when they break from the herd, we do.

It's risky to say "no" to something others easily accept or vice versa. To walk out of a movie when you realize you don't want those words or images to become part of your memory. To accept responsibility for a mistake, instead of "stretching the truth" about what really happened. To stand up for what you believe, even when you know you might be misunderstood or ridiculed. To choose to forgive what others may label "unforgivable."

Following God sometimes means following a different path than those around us. But wherever God leads, He goes with us...guiding us, strengthening us and giving us the courage and wisdom we need to become the people He's created us to be.

Be strong and of a good courage; be not afraid,
neither be thou dismayed:
for the Lord thy God is with thee
whithersoever thou goest.
Joshua 1:9

Two roads diverged in a wood, and I—
I took the one less traveled by,
And that has made all the difference.
Robert Frost

To be yourself in a world that is constantly trying
to make you something else is the greatest
accomplishment.
Ralph Waldo Emerson

Faith is the daring of the soul
to go farther than it can see.
William Newton Clarke

I WOULD RATHER BE WHAT GOD CHOSE TO MAKE
ME THAN THE MOST GLORIOUS CREATURE THAT
I COULD THINK OF; FOR TO HAVE BEEN THOUGHT
ABOUT, BORN IN GOD'S THOUGHT, AND THEN
MADE BY GOD, IS THE DEAREST, GRANDEST AND
MOST PRECIOUS THING IN ALL THINKING.
GEORGE MACDONALD

If man does not keep pace with his companions,
perhaps it is because he hears
a different drummer.
Henry David Thoreau

TRUST IN THE LORD WITH ALL THINE HEART;
AND LEAN NOT UNTO THINE OWN
UNDERSTANDING.
IN ALL THY WAYS ACKNOWLEDGE HIM,
AND HE SHALL DIRECT THY PATHS.
PROVERBS 3:5-6

FAINTHEARTED GOATS?

Fainting goats are not faint of heart. Actually, they don't even live up to their name. They don't faint. They have a hereditary condition called Thomsen's disease. When they're startled, their bodies tense up for 10 to 20 seconds and can't relax. It's like a full-body charley horse, without the pain. When this happens, they tip over. Thankfully, as the goats mature they adapt to their medical condition and are able to remain upright.

Also referred to as "nervous goats" or "Tennessee wooden-legs," this unique breed is known for their easy-going, laid back personality. Every October they are honored at the Goats, Music and More Festival in Tennessee, which features a goat rodeo and the World Grand Champion Fainting Goats Show.

THE MIRACLE OF YOU

Our bodies are amazingly diverse and complex. One tiny glitch in our DNA or the intricate systems God's designed to keep our bodies functioning and things go awry. Just like fainting goats. When we're healthy, we rarely consider that every breath, every beat of our heart and every individual thought is such a priceless gift. Only when our health is compromised in some way, do we gain a true appreciation of the miracle that is "our body."

Take some time today to thank God for little things you may often take for granted. Your fingers. Your eyelids. Your taste buds. Your ability to literally stop and smell the roses. If you're struggling with physical issues, talk to God about those, as well. His attention to detail in creating us and every other amazing creature that lives on this earth, shows He cares about every aspect of our lives, big or small. If it matters to us, it matters to Him.

I will praise thee;
for I am fearfully and wonderfully made...
Psalm 139:14

IN ALL THINGS OF NATURE THERE
IS SOMETHING OF THE MARVELOUS.
ARISTOTLE

God cares about the BIG things, the small things,
and ALL things in your life.

IS ANY AMONG YOU AFFLICTED? LET HIM PRAY.
IS ANY MERRY? LET HIM SING PSALMS.
JAMES 5:13

Look at your health;
and if you have it, praise God,
and value it next to a good conscience.
Izaak Walton

TEACH US TO NUMBER OUR DAYS, THAT WE MAY
APPLY OUR HEARTS UNTO WISDOM.
PSALM 90:12

Seeing, hearing, feeling, are miracles,
and each part and tag of me is a miracle.
Walt Whitman

WE ARE THE CLAY, AND THOU OUR POTTER;
AND WE ALL ARE THE WORK OF THY HAND.
ISAIAH 64:8

THE PANDA PARADOX

The giant panda is easily recognizable. It's the bear that's black and white, right? Well, kinda. There's still discussion as to which "family" of animals pandas should be classified with: bear or raccoon. On a molecular level, the giant panda is a bear. But they're odd bears. They don't hibernate. Instead of roaring (in true ursine fashion), they bleat and honk. Their digestive system is suited to bearlike carnivores, yet 99% of their diet is bamboo.

The giant panda (along with primates and one very odd frog) is also one of few animals to have an opposable thumb. Kinda. Along with its five fingers, the panda uses its enlarged wrist bone (a pseudo-thumb) to grasp bamboo stalks. Since the giant panda needs to consume at least 30 pounds of bamboo every day, it requires a large amount of "personal space" to supply its nutritional needs. Consequently, pandas lead solitary lives.

THE GRAY ZONE

Differentiating between right and wrong is kind of like trying to classify a panda bear. It's not black and white. Take lying. It's wrong! Right? But what about those during World War II who hid Jews in their homes and lied about it?

Granted, most questionable decisions we have to make are of lesser consequence. But that doesn't mean we should adopt the motto: If it feels good, do it. Our feelings are not the best barometer of what's right. We need to weigh what we feel against what God has to say.

In the Bible, Jesus tells us to love God and love others. That's the best measuring stick we have to evaluate "gray areas" in our lives. In addition, God's provided us with a conscience, critical thinking skills, experience, the counsel of those we respect and prayer. Put them all together and we're ready to make a decision. Then, all that's left to do is the right thing.

Every day the choice between good and evil is
presented to us in simple ways.
William Edwin Sangster

THE WAYS OF THE LORD ARE RIGHT,
AND THE JUST SHALL WALK IN THEM.
HOSEA 14:9

Right is right even if no one is doing it; wrong is
wrong even if everyone is doing it.
Augustine of Hippo

NEVER TIRE IN DOING WHAT IS GOOD.
2 THESSALONIANS 3:13 NIV

Obedience means marching right on whether we feel like it or not. Many times we go against our feelings. Faith is one thing, feeling another.
D. L. Moody

LOVE THE LORD THY GOD WITH ALL THY HEART, AND WITH ALL THY SOUL, AND WITH ALL THY MIND. THIS IS THE FIRST AND GREAT COMMANDMENT. AND THE SECOND IS LIKE UNTO IT, THOU SHALT LOVE THY NEIGHBOR AS THYSELF. ON THESE TWO COMMANDMENTS HANG ALL THE LAW AND THE PROPHETS.
MATTHEW 22:37-40

Never, for the sake of peace and quiet, deny your own experience or convictions.
Dag Hammarskjöld

WHEN SHEEP GO ON THE LAM

A group of sheep is known as a herd, a flock or a mob. It's easy to picture why they earned that last name. If one sheep starts running, all of those nearby follow suit. It doesn't matter where that one sheep is headed. That's where they all want to go. But if sheep panic, all bets are off. Frightened sheep scatter every which way, like a jar of marbles dropped on a hardwood floor.

That's why sheep need a sheepdog or a shepherd to keep the flock together and headed in the right direction. Sheep aren't stupid, as some people tend to believe. They're simply skittish—and defenseless. They depend on people to lead them, feed them and protect them from danger. As domesticated animals, one of the very earliest to be bred and raised in ways that make them dependent on man, sheep can't survive long on their own. We depend on them for wool and food and they depend on us to keep them safe.

WHERE HE LEADS, WE'LL FOLLOW

Sheep are no longer regarded as "wild" animals, but all domesticated animals were at one time off on their own. Just like us. When we choose to follow God as our Shepherd—instead of continuing to follow our own wild and woolly ways—we find the same type of order, protection and purpose that sheep do when they're under the safekeeping of a devoted caregiver.

Although many animals are mentioned throughout the Bible, sheep are the most prevalent. They're also commonly used as a synonym for God's children. Psalm 95:7 says, "He is our God; and we are the people of his pasture, and the sheep of his hand." The Bible reassures us that God is a good shepherd. He won't lead us astray. We do that well enough on our own.

Being dependent on God isn't a sign of weakness. It's a sign of wisdom. When we listen for His voice, and follow where He leads, we can relax. We know that whatever we encounter in "his pasture," we never face it alone.

The Lord is my shepherd; I shall not want.
He maketh me to lie down in green pastures:
he leadeth me beside the still waters.
He restoreth my soul.
Psalm 23:1-3

THERE IS NEVER A FEAR THAT HAS NOT
A CORRESPONDING "FEAR NOT."
AMY WILSON CARMICHAEL

Fear not: for I have redeemed thee, I have called
thee by thy name; thou art mine.
Isaiah 43:1

YOU DO NOT HAVE TO CHANGE GOD'S WILL OR
MAKE GOD CHANGE HIS MIND TOWARDS YOU,
BUT ONLY TO BECOME CHANGED YOURSELF,
IN ORDER TO BE MADE AT-ONE,
OR BROUGHT IN TUNE, WITH THE GOOD THAT
GOD HAS PREPARED FOR YOU.
HENRY THOMAS HAMBLIN

He calleth his own sheep by name.
John 10:3

By confronting us with irreducible
mysteries that stretch our daily vision to
include infinity, nature opens an inviting
and guiding path toward a spiritual life.
Thomas More

Jesus, when he came out, saw much people,
and was moved with compassion toward them,
because they were as sheep not having a
shepherd: and he began to teach them.
Mark 6:34

I am the good shepherd; the good shepherd
giveth his life for the sheep.
John 10:11

SLOTHS TAKE IT SLOW

Sloths have been made fun of ever since they were discovered. When Spanish explorers found them in the rainforests of South America, they placed their tongue firmly in their cheek and named the world's slowest mammal, "Nimble Peter."

How slow is a sloth? A female sloth moving at top speed to help her endangered child can travel about 14 feet per minute. But most of the time, a sloth takes a minute to move just a few inches. It was once believed sloths slept almost 20 hours a day. The truth is, they sleep about nine. They just move so infrequently researchers thought they were sleeping.

But the sloth's lack of speed actually works to its advantage. It's nearly imperceptible movement, and the algae that consequently grows in its fur, help camouflage the sloth from predators. This is God's natural security system, since sloths lack the ability to flee.

THE REST OF THE STORY

It sounds rather judgmental to label an animal slothful or lazy just because it moves at the speed God intended it to. But if we're honest with ourselves, we're prone to judge people the same way explorers judged the sloth— by what's seen at first glance.

We may not say it aloud, but our inner voice often pronounces judgment on those around us. We judge them by how they drive, how they parent, how much they weigh, what they're wearing...and on and on.

But we don't know the whole story. We don't know their personal history and current circumstances. We aren't privy to the unique way God's designed their brain and their body. We only know them from the outside. God knows them from the inside out. He's the only one qualified to judge us, and our actions, because He's the only one who sees us as we really are.

Believe me, every man has his secret sorrows,
which the world knows not; and oftentimes we
call a man cold, when he is only sad.
Henry Wadsworth Longfellow

GOD EXAMINES BOTH RICH AND POOR, NOT
ACCORDING TO THEIR LANDS AND HOUSES, BUT
ACCORDING TO THE RICHES OF THEIR HEARTS.
AUGUSTINE OF HIPPO

Judge not, that ye be not judged.
Matthew 7:1

IT WE HAD NO FAULTS, WE SHOULD TAKE SO
MUCH PLEASURE IN NOTICING THOSE OF OTHERS.
FRANÇOIS DE LA ROCHEFOUCAULD

Don't rely too much on labels,
Far too often they are fables.
Charles Haddon Spurgeon

BE GENTLE WITH JUDGEMENT
OF THOSE YOU MEET, FOR YOU NEVER KNOW
THE BURDENS THEY CARRY.

How rarely we weigh our neighbor in the same
balance in which we weigh ourselves.
Thomas à Kempis

IF YOU JUDGE PEOPLE,
YOU HAVE NO TIME TO LOVE THEM.
MOTHER TERESA

FOXES...THE FELINE CANINE

Though foxes are classified as wild dogs, they have a lot of cat-like qualities. They're the only dogs with retractable claws. They can climb trees—the only dogs in North America with that ability. The pupils of their eyes are vertical, making them appear more feline than canine. Foxes also play with their prey before killing it. Just like cats.

Most wild dogs live in packs. Not foxes. Like the majority of cats, foxes are solitary animals. That is, unless it's breeding season or they're raising their kits. (Sounds a bit like "kittens," don't you think?) Though the eyesight of foxes is weak, they have an acute sense of smell and hearing. It's been shown that foxes can hear the squeak of a mouse from 160 feet away. Talk about a feline canine!

It's Better Together

It's fine for a fox to live a solitary life. But the same isn't true for us. God designed people to live in community. As babies, we're dependent on those around us to help fill our every need. As we grow, our need becomes less visible, but that doesn't mean it's less necessary.

Strong relationships have been shown to benefit us mentally, physically and emotionally. Not only is the companionship of others enjoyable, it makes us stronger as a community. That's because every individual has talents, skills, experience and insight that differs from any other human being who's ever walked the face of the earth.

This means you are invaluable and irreplaceable. The world wouldn't be the same without you. Literally. So be part of it. Reach out for help when you need it. Reach out to help others when you can. Risk making new friends. Attend to relationships in need of repair. Think of life in terms of "us," instead of just "me." Community is a gift we give one another.

No man is an island entire of itself.
John Donne

MAN IS A SPECIAL BEING, AND IF LEFT TO HIMSELF,
IN AN ISOLATED CONDITION, WOULD BE ONE OF
THE WEAKEST CREATURES; BUT ASSOCIATED WITH
HIS KIND, HE WORKS WONDERS.
DANIEL WEBSTER

What do we live for,
if it is not to make life less difficult
for each other?
George Eliot

THIS IS MY COMMANDMENT,
THAT YE LOVE ONE ANOTHER,
AS I HAVE LOVED YOU.
JOHN 15:12

As we have therefore opportunity,
let us do good unto all men.
Galatians 6:10

MAKE IT A RULE, AND PRAY TO GOD TO HELP
YOU KEEP IT, NEVER, IF POSSIBLE, TO LIE DOWN
AT NIGHT WITHOUT BEING ABLE TO SAY:
"I HAVE MADE ONE HUMAN BEING AT LEAST
A LITTLE WISER, OR A LITTLE HAPPIER,
OR AT LEAST A LITTLE BETTER THIS DAY."
CHARLES KINGSLEY

We are all dependent on one another,
every soul of us on earth.
George Bernard Shaw

A MAN IS LIKE A LETTER OF THE ALPHABET:
TO PRODUCE A WORD,
IT MUST COMBINE WITH ANOTHER.
BENJAMIN MANDELSTAMM

RHINOS WHO SEE RED

Rhinos have big bodies and small brains. They weigh more than a ton, run at over 25 mph and have horrible eyesight. They can't distinguish a person from a tree from 15 feet away. They've even been known to charge rocks, mistaking them for predators. It's no wonder a group of rhinos is called a "crash."

Rhinos, particularly black rhinos, are notorious for their bad tempers. But you have to wonder whether they're aggression is related to their poor vision. They can't tell if something is friend or foe—or tree—until they're right on top of it.

Whatever the reason, black rhinos have the highest death rate of any animal for fighting with their own species: 50% of males and 30% of females die from these confrontations. Which raises the question: wouldn't a good pair of glasses go a long way in keeping rhinos off the endangered species list?

TAMING YOUR INNER RHINO

God has provided us with big brains and (more often than not) fairly decent eyesight. But there are times when we still go the way of the rhino. We charge off in anger before we totally understand why we're on the attack.

Instead of our feet, it's usually our tongues that race out of control. Before we risk endangering a relationship with hasty words we can never erase, it's important to slow down and look carefully at the situation. Just like rhinos, our aggression is often born out of fear. They're afraid of predators. We're afraid of being embarrassed, being inconvenienced or being ill-treated. Or maybe we've just had too little sleep, too much caffeine or are stressed out over something else altogether.

Whatever the cause, anger is rarely the best solution when it comes to solving a problem. So, when you feel your inner rhino starting to charge, take a deep breath. Hold your tongue. Ask God to help you see the situation clearly and clear-headedly. Then, proceed forward with caution, wisdom and grace.

He that is slow to wrath is
of great understanding.
Proverbs 14:29

PEOPLE WHO FLY INTO A RAGE
ALWAYS MAKE A BAD LANDING.
WILL ROGERS

My dear brothers and sisters, take note of this:
Everyone should be quick to listen,
slow to speak and slow to become angry,
because human anger does not produce
the righteousness that God desires.
James 1:19-20 NIV

HE THAT OVERCOMES HIS ANGER
CONQUERS HIS GREATEST ENEMY.
PROVERB

The trouble with letting off steam is that it only
gets you in more hot water.
Anonymous

KIND WORDS PRODUCE THEIR
OWN IMAGE IN MEN'S SOULS;
AND A BEAUTIFUL IMAGE IT IS.
BLAISE PASCAL

Speak when you are angry and you will make
the best speech you will ever regret.
Ambrose Bierce

THE BEST REMEDY FOR ANGER
IS A LITTLE TIME FOR THOUGHT.
SENECA

THE INSECT PROPHET

The praying mantis isn't the cuddliest of creatures. As a matter of fact, its triangular head, twig-like appendages and big, bug eyes give it kind of a science fiction villain look. The fact that it only has one ear (which is located on its belly), doesn't make the insect any more appealing. But because of its prayer-like stance, the praying mantis has received a lot of attention over the years.

The word "mantis" comes from the Greek word for prophet. In Africa, it's believed the insect can help find lost sheep and goats. In France, there's an old wives' tale that a praying mantis will actually guide a lost child back home. But just because the insect looks like it's praying doesn't mean it is. What it's actually doing is waiting in its "preying" position. Perhaps it's like an insect version of saying grace before an upcoming meal.

QUALITY TIME

As kids, we wish upon falling stars or birthday candles, hoping they have the power to make our fondest dreams come true. At times, we do the same thing with God. We talk to God when we want something or when life isn't turning out the way we'd planned. We present our "wish list" to Him and wait.

The longer we wait for an answer, the more we question ourselves and God. Is He really listening? Did we say the right words? Should we try praying "harder"? Mimic a "praying mantis" position? Ask someone holier than we are to talk to God on our behalf?

In this world of texting, tweeting and high speed internet, we're used to getting an instant response. But God's timing, and His answers, are so different from ours. Instead of a "wish list," consider prayer "quality time" with Someone you love. Freely share your heart. Place every thought and concern in God's Hands. Then trust Him to do with them whatever He sees as best.

Certain thoughts are prayers.
There are moments when,
whatever be the attitude of the body,
the soul is on its knees.
Victor Hugo

ANYTHING LARGE ENOUGH
FOR A WISH TO LIGHT UPON IS LARGE ENOUGH
TO HANG A PRAYER UPON.
GEORGE MACDONALD

The Spirit helps us in our weakness. We do not
know what we ought to pray for,
but the Spirit himself intercedes for us through
wordless groans.
Romans 8:26 NIV

TO PRAY IS TO MOUNT ON EAGLE'S WINGS ABOVE
THE CLOUDS AND GET INTO THE CLEAR HEAVEN
WHERE GOD DWELLETH.
CHARLES HADDON SPURGEON

Before they call, I will answer; and while they
are yet speaking, I will hear.
Isaiah 65:24

I KNOW NOT BY WHAT METHODS RARE,
BUT THIS I KNOW: GOD ANSWERS PRAYER...
I KNOW NOT IF THE BLESSING SOUGHT
WILL COME IN JUST THE WAY I THOUGHT.
BUT LEAVE MY PRAYERS WITH HIM ALONE
WHOSE WILL IS WISER THAN MY OWN...
ELIZA M. HICKOK

Pray without ceasing.
1 Thessalonians 5:17

KEEP PRAYING, BUT BE THANKFUL THAT GOD'S
ANSWERS ARE WISER THAN YOUR PRAYERS!
WILLIAM CULBERTSON

TIGER TIPS

How can you spot a happy tiger? They can't purr like a house cat to let you know they're in a good mood. Instead, you need to look for one that's squinting or has its eyes closed. Any cat that shuts its eyes (excluding those taking a bona-fide cat nap) is willingly lowering its vigilance and defenses. That means it feels safe and relaxed.

Tigers are such powerful hunters that they have no natural enemies. (Besides man and bacteria, that is). Their chosen hunting method is the "surprise attack," which is why a group of tigers is called an "ambush."

So, if you happen to cross paths with a tiger outside the zoo–and it isn't squint-ing–look it in the eyes. Once the element of surprise is gone, tigers are less likely to attack. That's why in some parts of India, it was once a common practice for people to wear a mask depicting a face on the back of their heads when walking through the jungle. Sometimes, it's safer to have eyes in the back of your head!

SAVOR THE SMALL STUFF

Even tigers have their happy place. When was the last time you visited yours? You don't have to be on vacation, get a promotion or have everything going your way to experience joy. All you need to do is to learn to savor the small stuff.

If your heart feels heavy, if you're dreading what lies ahead or mourning the end of what lies behind, take a break and go on a treasure hunt. God weaves beauty, blessing and wonder into each and every new day. Can you find it?

Refuse to allow the familiarity of routine, the roller coaster of getting older, or the uncertainty of circumstances to define your mood–or your life. Shift your focus. Instead of merely counting your blessings, thank God for each one. Bask in the blessing of being loved. Delight in God's artistry in the natural world. Relish a good meal, a good book or good conversation. As your gratitude grows, your happiness quotient will follow suit.

This is the day which the Lord hath made;
we will rejoice and be glad in it.
Psalm 118:24

In every thing give thanks.
1 Thessalonians 5:18

A multitude of small delights
constitute happiness.
Charles Baudelaire

Happy is that people,
whose God is the Lord.
Psalm 144:15

We have within ourselves
Enough to fill the present day with joy,
And overspread the future years with hope.
William Wordsworth

THERE IS NOT ONE BLADE OF GRASS,
THERE IS NO COLOR IN THIS WORLD
THAT IS NOT INTENDED TO MAKE US REJOICE.
JOHN CALVIN

Our life is what our thoughts make it.
Marcus Aurelius

UNLESS WE THINK OF OTHERS
AND DO SOMETHING FOR THEM, WE MISS ONE
OF THE GREATEST SOURCES OF HAPPINESS.
RAY LYMAN WILBUR

The Perfect Otter Accessory

Who could help but delight in the sweet whiskery smile of a sea otter? The way their sleek silhouettes slip through the waves makes you want to join right in. And all that hype about how they're one of the few wild animals to use tools (they use rocks to crack open their personal seafood buffet) leads us to believe that they're smart, too. Sounds like a truly awesome animal, right?

There's more. These lucky critters have a built-in purse under each arm. Imagine the convenience! They use their baggy skin pouch to stow an afternoon snack or their favorite oyster-cracking rock. Considering they have to eat 25% of their body weight each day these little storage spaces come in very handy. God thinks of everything!

CACHE AND CARRY

So, if you had an underarm "otter" pouch, what would you keep in it? Pictures of your kids? Car keys? Reading glasses? Breath mints?

We carry quite the conglomeration of stuff with us as we go about our day. But it's nothing compared to the stuff we accumulate at home. We collect mementos from days gone by, knickknacks that catch our eye, clothing to suit every climate and changing mood and things we no longer need, want or even remember we have.

Storing, maintaining and keeping track of our stuff can be a big job. The more stuff we have, the bigger job it is. How long has it been since you made a clean sweep of what you own? Repair or throw away what's broken. Donate what you no longer use to those in need. Then, think carefully before you acquire anything else. Is it necessary? Are you trying to fill an emotional need with a physical object? Can you afford it...really? The less we own, the more time and resources we have available to use in other areas of our life.

Not what you possess but what you do with what
you have, determines your true worth.
Thomas Carlyle

THE ABILITY TO SIMPLIFY MEANS
TO ELIMINATE THE UNNECESSARY
SO THAT THE NECESSARY MAY SPEAK.
HANS HOFFMANN

A man's life consisteth not in the abundance
of the things which he possesseth.
Luke 12:15

THE SCULPTOR PRODUCES THE BEAUTIFUL STATUE
BY CHIPPING AWAY SUCH PARTS
OF THE MARBLE BLOCK AS ARE NOT
NEEDED — IT IS A PROCESS OF ELIMINATION.
ELBERT HUBBARD

Our life is frittered away by detail...
Simplify, simplify, simplify!
Henry David Thoreau

IT IS THE SWEET, SIMPLE THINGS OF LIFE WHICH
ARE THE REAL ONES AFTER ALL.
LAURA INGALLS WILDER

To crave more than you need—that is poverty.
Ivan N. Panin

IN THIS WORLD IT IS NOT WHAT WE TAKE UP,
BUT WHAT WE GIVE UP THAT MAKES US RICH.
HENRY WARD BEECHER

Welcome to the Parliament

Owls have long been associated with wisdom. The truth is, their upright posture, round heads and large eyes remind us of... well, us. No wonder we want to view them as clever. We even refer to a group of owls as a wisdom, a parliament or a study.

An owl's eyes are so large that if we had eyes in the same proportion to our bodies as owls do, they'd be the size of grapefruits. But owls are at a disadvantage. Their eyes don't move. This is why God gave them a neck that can swivel 270 degrees. In addition, many of the approximately 200 species of owls have asymmetrical ears. Their ears are different sizes and found at different heights on their head to improve their hearing. An owl's unique eyes and ears may not make it any wiser, but it certainly makes it a formidable foe when on the hunt for dinner.

Go Ahead and Ask

Not all owls hoot. Some screech, squawk, whistle, hiss and even bark. But it's the familiar cry of "Who? Who?" that most people associate with the owl family. Maybe that's what really makes the owl seem wise—it's always asking questions.

In human social circles, querying for clarification or more information is often discouraged. Perhaps it's because admitting we don't know it all in front of others feels like a sign of weakness. In truth, it's a sign of strength, humility and reality. No one knows it all, except God.

Having faith doesn't mean we no longer have questions. It simply means we trust that God holds the answers. Chances are pretty good we won't understand all of them. After all, the Creator of the universe obviously has a broader grasp on the big picture of life than we do. But we can continue to seek a deeper understanding through prayer, reading the Bible and asking questions of those who are farther down the path of faith than we are right now.

A wise old owl sat on an oak,
The more he saw the less he spoke;
The less he spoke the more he heard;
Why aren't we like that wise old bird?
Edward Hersey Richards

I WOULD RATHER LIVE IN A WORLD
WHERE MY LIFE IS SURROUNDED BY MYSTERY
THAN LIVE IN A WORLD SO SMALL THAT
MY MIND COULD COMPREHEND IT.
HARRY EMERSON FOSDICK

How much better it is to get wisdom than gold!
and to get understanding rather
to be chosen than silver!
Proverbs 16:16

A WISE MAN IS ONE WHO HAS FINALLY
DISCOVERED THAT THERE ARE SOME QUESTIONS
TO WHICH NOBODY HAS THE ANSWER.
ANONYMOUS

The important thing is not to stop questioning.
Albert Einstein

JUDGE A MAN BY HIS QUESTIONS
RATHER THAN BY HIS ANSWERS.
VOLTAIRE

Wisdom is not finally tested in schools;
Wisdom cannot be pass'd from one having it,
to another not having it;
Wisdom is of the soul, is not susceptible of
proof, is its own proof.
Walt Whitman

ASK THE ANIMALS, AND THEY WILL TEACH YOU,
OR THE BIRDS IN THE SKY, AND THEY WILL TELL YOU;
OR SPEAK TO THE EARTH, AND IT WILL TEACH YOU,
OR LET THE FISH IN THE SEA INFORM YOU.
WHICH OF ALL THESE DOES NOT KNOW THAT
THE HAND OF THE LORD HAS DONE THIS?
IN HIS HAND IS THE LIFE OF EVERY CREATURE
AND THE BREATH OF ALL MANKIND.
JOB 12:7-10 NIV

Wombats Won't Give Up

Wombats are cute little critters...from a distance. Native to Australia, these furry marsupials look like a cross between a bear and an oversized guinea pig. Like their relative the koala bear, wombats have a rear-facing pouch where they keep their pea-sized newborn. This keeps the "nursery" from getting dirty when mom is busy digging. And can she ever dig!

Nicknamed Bulldozer of the Bush, wombats would rather go through than around. They can out dig a man with a shovel, especially in rock hard soil. The world's largest burrowing animal, wombats have been known to dig through walls and doors, anything that gets in their way. People used to believe this was because wombats were simple-minded, but actually they have the most developed brain of any marsupial. They're just tenacious. When they have a path in mind, they don't give up.

THE STAIRCASE TO SUCCESS

When we know which direction we should go, but there's an obstacle in our way, we need to take a lesson from the wombat. Don't give up. What looks like a solid wall can become a door with hard work and perseverance!

What's your personal Great Wall? Maybe you're trying to lose weight or get yourself out of debt. Or perhaps you want to earn a college degree or write the book that's been niggling in your mind for years. Whatever your goal, the only way to get there is to keep going.

When it comes to a long-term endeavor, our biggest obstacle is often mental. Help keep discouragement at bay by thinking about your "wall" in a different way. First, remind yourself why you're doing what you're doing. What's the purpose worthy of all of this hard work? Then, view every day as one step on a staircase that leads you to that end result. God's there with you, every step of the way. How high will you scale that staircase today?

Perseverance is not a long race;
it is many short races one after another.
Walter Elliott

LET US RUN WITH PERSEVERANCE THE RACE
MARKED OUT FOR US.
HEBREWS 12:1 NIV

By perseverance the snail reached the Ark.
Charles Haddon Spurgeon

OUR MOTTO MUST CONTINUE
TO BE PERSEVERANCE.
AND ULTIMATELY I TRUST THE ALMIGHTY
WILL CROWN OUR EFFORTS WITH SUCCESS.
WILLIAM WILBERFORCE

Be like a postage stamp—
stick to one thing until you get there.
Josh Billings

IN THE REALM OF IDEAS EVERYTHING
DEPENDS ON ENTHUSIASM; IN THE REAL WORLD,
ALL RESTS ON PERSEVERANCE.
JOHANN VON GOETHE

We conquer by continuing.
George Matheson

LET US NOT BE WEARY IN WELL DOING:
FOR IN DUE SEASON WE SHALL REAP.
GALATIANS 6:9

HOME TWEET HOME

When it comes to bachelor pads, the male bowerbird refuses to settle for a basic bird's nest. After constructing a complex frame of twigs on the rainforest floor, these birds decorate their one-of-a-kind homes with whatever catches their eye: leaves, moss, shells, berries, feathers, tinfoil, buttons, batteries, CDs...you name it. If a single, decorative flower petal shifts, the finicky bowerbird will return it to its original place.

But all of this work isn't just so the bowerbird can enjoy the ultimate man cave. It's all for the ladies. After a song and dance routine, male bowerbirds invite the females to visit their homes. Females fly from bower to bower to find one they like. After mating with the winning avian architect, the females head to a nearby tree and build their own unadorned nest where they'll raise the kids. As for the male, he'll go back to gussying up his not-so-humble abode.

More Than Just a Pretty Face

We're attracted to what's attractive. And, like bowerbirds, sometimes we go out of our way to make our surroundings (and ourselves) attractive to others. There's nothing wrong with that. After all, God has hard-wired us to be drawn to what's beautiful. He's woven threads of color, splendor and originality into each and every one of His creations, including bowerbirds—and us.

But as we incorporate beauty into our lives, let's remember that it really is more than skin deep. It doesn't matter if our house is perfect, our hair well-coiffed, our clothes in style and our eyebrows plucked if our heart is cold and our words are hard. What people are most attracted to are qualities like love, kindness, compassion and humility. When someone's heart displays qualities like these, others are naturally drawn to them. They're attractive in the most literal, wonderful, sense of the word.

Today, when you look in the mirror, take a moment to reflect on your inner beauty. Ask God to help make you more attractive where it really counts.

Beauty may be said to be
God's trademark in creation.
Henry Ward Beecher

YOUR BEAUTY SHOULD NOT COME FROM
OUTWARD ADORNMENT, SUCH AS ELABORATE
HAIRSTYLES AND THE WEARING OF
GOLD JEWELRY OR FINE CLOTHES. RATHER,
IT SHOULD BE THAT OF YOUR INNER SELF,
THE UNFADING BEAUTY OF A GENTLE
AND QUIET SPIRIT, WHICH IS OF GREAT
WORTH IN GOD'S SIGHT.
1 PETER 3:3–4 NIV

I pray, O God, that I may be beautiful within.
Socrates

A MERRY HEART DOETH
GOOD LIKE A MEDICINE.
PROVERBS 17:22

Though we travel the world over
to find the beautiful, we must carry it
with us or we find it not.
Ralph Waldo Emerson

In all ranks of life the human heart
yearns for the beautiful;
and the beautiful things that God
makes are his gift to all alike.
Harriet Beecher Stowe

Let the beauty of the Lord our God be upon us:
and establish thou the work of our hands.
Psalm 90:17

Beauty is God's handwriting...
Welcome it in every fair face,
every fair sky, every fair flower.
Charles Kingsley

A Penguin's Cry

Penguins are the opposite of the proverbial lone wolf. They like crowds, connection and community. They're often found in breeding colonies with tens of thousands of other penguins. Within these rookeries are individual families, most of them monogamous. Each family unit is its own little community which fulfills specific shared responsibilities.

Instead of building a nest, many species of penguin dads incubate a single egg on top of their feet for several months. During this time, mom is away at sea, fattening up. Shortly after the chicks hatch, the moms return and switch duties with the dads—who now head off to sea to replenish their stores of fat to help keep them warm and healthy.

Though a mass of penguins may all look alike to us, parents and chicks can find each other in a crowd of thousands. Each penguin has a distinct call, instantly recognizable by its family members. Luckily, they also have very acute hearing so they can hear that cry above the roar of the crowd.

God Knows Your Voice

There are more than 7 billion people in the world right now. Though not every corner of the globe is packed together as tightly as a penguin colony, it's easy to view humanity the same way we do a multitude of penguins: as a generic mass, instead of as individuals.

It's also easy to believe God views us the same way. Imagine having 7 billion children. And those are just the ones alive right now! Sure, God loves the world as a whole. But does He love each one of us individually? Can He tell our voices apart when we pray?

When Jesus was on earth, He didn't simply address the crowds from a distance. He spoke to people one-on-one. He comforted them. He prayed for them. He loved them. And He loves us. The Bible assures us that God knows each one of us by name. He hears our prayers as clearly as if we were the only one speaking. Like the penguin, God can recognize our cry above the crowd. And He promises to answer when we call.

He prayeth best, who loveth best
All things both great and small;
For the dear God who loveth us,
He made and loveth all.
Samuel Taylor Coleridge

GOD LOVES EACH OF US AS
IF THERE WERE ONLY ONE OF US.
AUGUSTINE OF HIPPO

The LORD your God is with you,
the Mighty Warrior who saves.
He will take great delight in you;
in his love he will no longer rebuke you,
but will rejoice over you with singing.
Zephaniah 3:17 NIV

GOD ENTERS BY A PRIVATE DOOR
INTO EVERY INDIVIDUAL.
RALPH WALDO EMERSON

Call unto me, and I will answer thee, and show
thee great and mighty things,
which thou knowest not.
Jeremiah 33:3

HE WHO COUNTS THE STARS
AND CALLS THEM BY THEIR NAMES,
IS IN NO DANGER OF FORGETTING
HIS OWN CHILDREN. HE KNOWS YOUR
CASE AS THOROUGHLY AS IF YOU WERE
THE ONLY CREATURE HE EVER MADE,
OR THE ONLY SAINT HE EVER LOVED.
CHARLES HADDON SPURGEON

In my distress I cried unto the Lord,
and he heard me.
Psalm 120:1

THE LOVE OF CHRIST IS LIKE THE BLUE SKY,
INTO WHICH YOU MAY SEE CLEARLY,
BUT THE REAL VASTNESS OF WHICH
YOU CANNOT MEASURE.
ROBERT MURRAY MCCHEYNE

TWIN-TONGUED BUSH BABIES

Bush babies are tiny African primates that weigh less than a pound. Though they're only five inches tall, they can leap like furry frogs! They're able to jump over six feet straight up into the air and over twenty feet when leaping from tree to tree.

Large round eyes and big ears make bush babies look like a cross between a monkey and a meerkat. But they have something very unique in the animal world—a second tongue. Primarily used for grooming their long, thick fur, this second tongue is located directly beneath the first.

Also known as galagos or nagapies, bush babies received their common name from British explorers who thought their cries sounded just like excited children. No word as to whether a second tongue would help human children sound more like bush babies...

GROOM YOUR WORDS

One tiny, little tongue can cause a lot of damage. That's because, unlike bush babies, we don't use our tongue for grooming. We use it for forming words. Words can be wonderful things. They can be used to paint a picture through story, poetry or song. They can lift someone's spirits or soothe a troubled soul. They can offer directions, instruction or prayer. They can help us reveal more of who we are to someone we love.

But when we're careless with our words— when we speak before we think—words can just as easily be used to twist the truth, break someone's heart or build walls (instead of bridges) between ourselves and those around us.

Want to use your tongue wisely? Stop and listen. Give your full attention to the person speaking. Ask questions. Thoughtfully consider their answers. Then, stop long enough to consider what you're going to say—and why. Take a lesson from the bush baby and groom your words before allowing them to leap off your tongue.

The tongue of the wise useth knowledge aright.
Proverbs 15:2

A SPOKEN WORD IS NOT A SPARROW.
ONCE IT FLIES OUT YOU CAN'T CATCH IT.
PROVERB

A word fitly spoken is like apples of gold
in pictures of silver.
Proverbs 25:11

OUR WORDS ARE A FAITHFUL INDEX OF THE
STATE OF OUR SOULS.
FRANCIS DE SALES

There is not a word in my tongue,
but, lo, O Lord, thou knowest it altogether.
Psalm 139:4

Speaking without thinking
is shooting without aiming.
Sir William Gurney Benham

The tongue weighs practically nothing,
yet so few people can hold it!
Anonymous

A wholesome tongue is a tree of life.
Proverbs 15:4

THE HYPERACTIVE HUMMINGBIRD

Flying Jewels...that's what early explorers to the New World named hummingbirds. Modern ornithologists obviously agreed, giving some of the over 300 species names like: Amethyst Woodstar, Crimson Topaz and Glittering-Bellied Emerald.

Known for their iridescent plumage, diminutive size and incredible speed, hummingbirds are always on the go. To maintain their high energy lifestyle, they need to eat twice their body weight every day, which means visiting hundreds of flowers in search of nectar and small insects. Unfortunately, hummingbirds can't stop and smell the roses. First, they don't have the ability to smell. Second, their feet are so tiny they can't walk on the ground.

But hummingbirds sure can fly. They can reach speeds of 25–50 mph if they're performing a courtship dive! They can also fly backwards, sideways, hover in mid-air and fly short distances upside-down. Not only are they flying jewels, they're avian acrobats.

THE NEW YOU

Hummingbirds are the only birds that can fly backwards. People can't fly without assistance from a hang glider or jumbo jet. However, God has given us hummingbird-like ability to back up and head a new direction at will.

We can't change the past, but we can change the course of our future. With God's help, we can break old habits. We can reassess longstanding opinions. We can apply for a different job. We can forgive what seems unpardonable—in others, as well as in ourselves. God does.

There's nothing in our past that is so big, or so bad, that it can separate us from God's love and care. He invites us to draw close to Him in prayer. To trust Him with our deepest secrets. In return, he not only offers us forgiveness, but a fresh start. If you're headed the wrong direction, there's no better time to turn around than right now. Allow God to help transform you into the amazing individual He created you to be.

If any man be in Christ, he is a new creature:
old things are passed away;
behold, all things are become new.
2 Corinthians 5:17

GOD LOVES HIS CHILDREN RIGHT
WHERE THEY ARE, AND HE SHINES A SPECIAL
LIGHT TO HELP THEM MOVE AHEAD.

He that cannot forgive others breaks the bridge
over which he must pass himself; for every man
has need to be forgiven.
Thomas Fuller

BE YE KIND ONE TO ANOTHER,
TENDERHEARTED, FORGIVING ONE ANOTHER,
EVEN AS GOD FOR CHRIST'S SAKE
HATH FORGIVEN YOU.
EPHESIANS 4:32

You cannot prevent the birds of sadness from
passing over your head, but you can prevent
their making a nest in your hair.
Proverb

And the humming-bird that hung
Like a jewel up among
The tilted honeysuckle horns
They mesmerized and swung
In the palpitating air,
Drowsed with odors strange and rare.
And, with whispered laughter, slipped away,
And left him hanging there.
James Whitcomb Riley

Change is the nursery
of music, joy, life and eternity.
John Donne

Behold, I make all things new.
And he said unto me, Write:
for these words are true and faithful.
Revelation 21:5

DOLPHINS TO THE RESCUE!

Dolphins are like the Florence Nightingale of the sea. They've been observed caring for the sick, injured and elderly. If one dolphin sends out a distress cry, other members of its pod will immediately come to its aid. If it's having trouble keeping its blow hole above the surface, the other dolphins will work together to keep it afloat.

Dolphin also act as midwives. When one of them is about to give birth, they surround the mother-to-be to keep her safe from predators. They've also been known to gently tug at the baby's tail to aid in its delivery and whistle what appears to be a song of encouragement to mother and child.

But dolphins don't reserve their support for members of their own pod. They've been known to come to the aid of humans in need of assistance, as well. How blessed we are to share this world with amazing creatures like these!

CHOOSE COMPASSION

Although we can't really understand what goes on in the heart of dolphins (emotionally, that is) their actions seem to convey a sense of compassion and camaraderie. When we reach out to help someone else, our actions convey that same message—whether our heart is totally onboard with our decision or not.

Helping others can be uncomfortable, inconvenient and costly in many regards. After all, anytime we put someone else's needs before our own, we sacrifice something. It may be our time, our resources or our comfort. It may even be all three. But that's what living a life of love is all about. When we love, we give.

Though love and compassion can be driven by emotion, they're just as often fueled by a black and white decision. We choose to reach out because there's a need we feel God wants us to fill. The more we listen, and act, on that tug at our heartstrings that urges us to come to the aid of others, the less of a sacrifice we'll feel we're making—and the more aware we'll be of the joy we receive in return.

Our worth is determined by the good deeds we
do, rather than by the fine emotions we feel.
Elias L. Magoon

WHAT DO WE LIVE FOR,
IF IT IS NOT TO MAKE LIFE LESS DIFFICULT
TO EACH OTHER?
GEORGE ELIOT

I have given you an example,
that ye should do as I have done to you.
John 13:15

BEHOLD,
I DO NOT GIVE LECTURES OR A LITTLE CHARITY,
WHEN I GIVE I GIVE MYSELF.
WALT WHITMAN

There is no better exercise for the heart than
reaching down and lifting people up.
John Andrew Holmes

CHRIST HAS NO BODY NOW ON EARTH BUT
YOURS, NO HANDS BUT YOURS,
NO FEET BUT YOURS, YOURS ARE THE EYES
THROUGH WHICH TO LOOK OUT
CHRIST'S COMPASSION TO THE WORLD
YOURS ARE THE FEET WITH WHICH HE IS
TO GO ABOUT DOING GOOD;
YOURS ARE THE HANDS WITH WHICH HE IS
TO BLESS MEN NOW.
TERESA OF ÁVILA

Be like-minded, be sympathetic,
love one another, be compassionate and humble.
1 Peter 3:8 NIV

NO ONE IS USELESS IN THIS WORLD WHO
LIGHTENS THE BURDEN OF IT FOR ANYONE ELSE.
CHARLES DICKENS

THE COOLEST OF CATERPILLARS

When you hear the word "caterpillar," chances are the one that first comes to mind is the wooly bear. It's one of the few caterpillars most people in North America instantly recognize. Its body is made up of thirteen segments covered with black and reddish brown fuzz. If you touch it, it curls up into a ball and plays dead—which is why it's nicknamed the "hedgehog caterpillar."

While most caterpillars only live for a couple of weeks before they begin their transformation into a butterfly, the wooly bear lives an entire year in its wormy state. That is, unless its home is the Arctic. Then its lifespan can extend to up to fourteen years. That's because the arctic wooly bear caterpillar spends 90% of its life frozen solid. Surviving temperatures that reach 70° below zero, it's only active a couple weeks out of each year when it eats like crazy. Eventually, like all wooly bear caterpillars, it will create a cocoon and begin its metamorphosis into an Isabella Tiger Moth.

Connecting to an Abundant Life

A long life is not synonymous with a full life. Just ask the wooly bear caterpillar. Who cares if you live to be one hundred if 90% of your time is spent cut off from, and oblivious to, the great big wonderful world around you?

God's plan for your life is for you to live in abundance. Not an abundance of stuff. Not the trappings of fortune and fame. But true abundance, the kind that fills your soul to overflowing. The kind that flows from the inside out.

This starts with connection: connecting to God and others through the lifeline of love. This connection doesn't happen by chance. It hinges on choice. You can remain as alone and aloof as a frozen woolly bear. Or, you can risk reaching out. Communicating honestly and openly with God, and with those He's placed in your life, helps connect you to a more abundant life—a life filled with passion, purpose and praise.

May you live all the days of your life.
Jonathan Swift

I CAME THAT THEY MIGHT HAVE LIFE, AND THAT
THEY MIGHT HAVE IT MORE ABUNDANTLY.
JOHN 10:10

Let every dawn of morning be to you as the
beginning of life and every setting sun be to you
as its close; then let every one of these short
lives leave its sure record of some kindly
thing done for others, some goodly strength
or knowledge gained for yourself.
John Ruskin

AS IS A TALE, SO IS LIFE: NOT HOW LONG IT IS,
BUT HOW GOOD IT IS, IS WHAT MATTERS.
SENECA

The value of life lies not in the length of days,
but in the use we make of them.
Michel de Montaigne

DO ALL THE GOOD YOU CAN, BY ALL THE MEANS
YOU CAN, IN ALL THE WAYS YOU CAN, IN ALL THE
PLACES YOU CAN, AT ALL THE TIMES YOU CAN, TO
ALL THE PEOPLE YOU CAN, AS LONG AS YOU CAN.
JOHN WESLEY

I must endure the presence
of a few caterpillars if I wish to become
acquainted with the butterflies.
Antoine de Saint-Exupéry

YOU WILL FIND AS YOU LOOK BACK UPON YOUR
LIFE THAT THE MOMENTS WHEN YOU HAVE
REALLY LIVED ARE THE MOMENTS WHEN YOU
HAVE DONE THINGS IN THE SPIRIT OF LOVE.
HENRY DRUMMOND

THE PATCHWORK PLATYPUS

The platypus sounds like a work of fiction. Found only in Australia, it has the bill and webbed feet of a duck, the fur and wide tail of a beaver and the reproductive system of a reptile. Platypus reproduction is also a bit tricky, since the males have sharp spurs on their hind feet containing toxic venom! Even platypus chromosomes are confused. Some are reptilian and some are mammalian.

The platypus has very poor eyesight. But that's of little consequence since it hunts in murky river water at night—with its eyes closed. It uses an electrosensory system to locate its prey (through tiny pits in its bill) and scoops the crustaceans and other invertebrates into its cheek pouches, which serve as grocery bags until it's ready to dine.

The platypus is such an enigma that the first scientists who examined the species first thought they were victims of a hoax. God's creativity knows no bounds!

BE YOUR OWN MIRROR

The platypus is an odd duck. (Or beaver or lizard or whatever you'd like to call it!) It seems a bit like an outlier in the animal kingdom. Have you ever felt that way, like you just don't fit in?

At one time or another, we've all felt like an outsider—like we don't know the secret handshake, don't possess the intelligence, the pedigree, the charisma or the supermodel good looks that seem to come naturally to those around us. Comparing ourselves with those we view as the "best and brightest" will always leave us feeling "less than..." The truth is that every person is like a platypus, a mixed bag of strengths and weaknesses, advantages and limitations. Comparing ourselves to others is like comparing a tiger with a toucan. One isn't better than the other. They're simply different.

God created us as individuals, one-of-a-kind works of art. Instead of comparing ourselves to others, let's compare who we are today with who we were last year and who we'd like to become in the year ahead. That's the only way to evaluate a masterpiece that isn't finished yet.

Every individual has a place to fill in the world,
and is important, in some respect,
whether he chooses to be so or not.
Nathaniel Hawthorne

WE ARE GOD'S HANDIWORK, CREATED IN
CHRIST JESUS TO DO GOOD WORKS, WHICH GOD
PREPARED IN ADVANCE FOR US TO DO.
EPHESIANS 2:10 NIV

Use what talents you possess:
the woods would be very silent if no birds sang
there except those that sang best.
Henry van Dyke

WE SHOULD HAVE GREAT PEACE
IF WE DID NOT BUSY OURSELVES WITH
WHAT OTHERS SAY AND DO.
THOMAS À KEMPIS

God has put something noble and good into
every heart which His hand created.
Mark Twain

EACH ONE SHOULD TEST THEIR OWN ACTIONS.
THEN THEY CAN TAKE PRIDE IN THEMSELVES
ALONE, WITHOUT COMPARING THEMSELVES TO
SOMEONE ELSE, FOR EACH ONE SHOULD CARRY
THEIR OWN LOAD.
GALATIANS 6:4–5 NIV

Most of us are like snowflakes trying to be like
each other, yet knowing full well that no two
snowflakes are ever identical. If we were to
devote the same amount of energy in trying to
discover the true self that lies buried deep within
our own nature, we would all work harmoniously
with life instead of forever *fighting* it.
Walter E. Elliott

WE FORFEIT THREE-FOURTHS OF OURSELVES
IN ORDER TO BE LIKE OTHER PEOPLE.
ARTHUR SCHOPENHAUER

SILVERBACK CELEBRITY

At first glance, gorillas seem like the animal kingdom's top choice for a "Find Me a Perfect Mate" reality show. Female gorillas carefully choose a silverback (a mature male, recognized by the silver hair covering its back) they want to follow for life. Each male is judged on his strength, size, good looks and leadership ability.

A silverback's "troop" isn't exclusive. It may include 10 (and at times up to 40!) females and their offspring. On occasion, other silverbacks may join the group. But there's no question as to who's in charge. When everyone is sitting around grooming one another, he's the one who's groomed—but doesn't stoop to grooming anyone else.

But the silverback's position isn't all fun and games. He resolves conflict within the troop. He's in charge of choosing favorable feeding grounds. Gentle with his family, but aggressive in the face of danger, the leader is ultimately responsible for the troop's safety. If necessary, he'll give his life defending those who've chosen to follow him.

LEADING WITH LOVE

When it comes to people, the best leaders aren't necessarily the biggest, strongest or best looking. They're the ones with a servant's heart. Unlike the gorilla, a great human leader will stoop down to "groom" others. That's exactly what Jesus did when He washed His disciples' feet. He was showing them—and us—that love leads best when serving others, instead of expecting to be served.

God has given each of us the ability to lead. We may lead a military unit into battle or a corporation toward success. Or not. We may lead in less visible (but not less significant) ways. Maybe we'll become a mentor, volunteer to head a ministry at church or guide our children toward maturity.

What does your "troop" need most? Encouragement? Feedback? A helping hand? If we spend less time on the soapbox and more time on our knees in prayer, we'll be more aware of what our team needs to succeed. Then, we can do our best to see those needs are met. We have a responsibility to those who follow us—not just to lead them in the right direction, but guide them there with grace, respect, humility and love.

You must be careful how you walk, and where
you go, for there are those following you who
will set their feet where yours are set.
Robert E. Lee

IF ANY MAN DESIRE TO BE FIRST,
THE SAME SHALL BE LAST OF ALL,
AND SERVANT OF ALL.
MARK 9:35

He that would be a leader must be a bridge.
Proverb

IT IS NOT FAIR TO ASK OF OTHERS WHAT YOU ARE
UNWILLING TO DO YOURSELF.
ELEANOR ROOSEVELT

A true and safe leader is likely to be one who
has no desire to lead...but will be humble,
gentle, self-sacrificing and altogether as ready to
follow as to lead.
A. W. Tozer

LET US BE SERVANTS IN ORDER TO BE LEADERS.
FYODOR DOSTOYEVSKY

Do nothing out of selfish ambition
or vain conceit. Rather, in humility
value others above yourselves.
Philippians 2:3 NIV

EXAMPLE IS NOT THE MAIN THING
IN INFLUENCING OTHERS. IT IS THE ONLY THING.
ALBERT SCHWEITZER

THE LION'S ACHILLES' HEEL

Lions are considered the only "social" feline. (Most housecats would unequivocally agree...) It's been said that the lion's social structure is closer to that of wolves and wild dogs than it is to other big cats. A pride of lions usually consists of one or two males, five females and their cubs. The pride hunts together, eats together, raises their cubs together and (at least for the females) stays together their entire lives.

Erroneously called the King of the Jungle, lions actually live in the grasslands and plains of Africa, as well as the Gir Forest of India. They can run 50 mph (for short distances) and leap 36 feet. Their unnerving roar can be heard from five miles away.

Who would have guessed this majestic hunter's worst enemy is—the porcupine. That's because lions check out their environment by sniffing. And when you sniff a porcupine, you can end up with quills stuck in your jaw for life. That's not only uncomfortable, but can interfere with eating, causing serious health issues.

BEWARE OF PORCUPINES

We all have porcupines in our lives, those seemingly little things that can bring us to our knees. Are you familiar with yours? Perhaps it's a penchant to spend just a tad more than you make. Maybe it's reading about those glamourous and successful celebrities that always leave you feeling a little dissatisfied with what you have. Or it could be that bakery right across from the gym where you've been working so hard to stay healthy.

The more familiar we are with our porcupines, the less likely we'll be to sidle right up to them and give them a sniff. We'll see them for what they really are: formidable foes best kept at a distance.

Areas of weakness in our lives are like battlefields. The farther we stay away from enemy lines, the fewer skirmishes (and potential defeats) we'll face. Sometimes, victory means being wise enough to walk away from a fight. So, don't head to the mall (with gold card in hand) when you're bored. Pick up a book that will change your life for the better. Switch gyms, if necessary! Choose to make your life a porcupine-free zone, whenever possible.

You must do the thing you think you cannot do.
Eleanor Roosevelt

WE SHOULD KEEP UP IN OUR HEARTS A
CONSTANT SENSE OF OUR OWN WEAKNESS,
NOT WITH A DESIGN TO DISCOURAGE THE MIND AN
DEPRESS THE SPIRITS, BUT WITH A VIEW
TO DRIVE US OUT OF OURSELVES IN SEARCH OF THE
DIVINE ASSISTANCE.
HANNAH MORE

The spirit truly is ready, but the flesh is weak.
Mark 14:38

THE PEOPLE WHO GET ON IN THIS WORLD
ARE THE PEOPLE WHO GET UP AND LOOK FOR THE
CIRCUMSTANCES THEY WANT, AND IF THEY
CAN'T FIND THEM, MAKE THEM.
GEORGE BERNARD SHAW

The road to success is dotted with
many tempting parking spaces.
Will Rogers

BE STRONG IN THE LORD,
AND IN THE POWER OF HIS MIGHT.
EPHESIANS 6:10

No temptation has overtaken you except
what is common to mankind.
And God is faithful; he will not let you be
tempted beyond what you can bear.
But when you are tempted, he will also provide
a way out so that you can endure it.
1 Corinthians 10:13 NIV

LET US LEARN MORE ABOUT THE POWER OF
TEMPTATION IN ORDER TO AVOID IT.
JOHN OWEN

EVERLASTING JELLIES

They look like graceful ballerinas dancing to a silent sonata, their tutus sporting every color of the rainbow. They're known by names like Blue Button, Flower Hat, Fried Egg and Darth Vader. Jellyfish may look ethereally beautiful, but the sting of the smallest jelly is 100 times more potent than cobra venom. Not that all jellies sting. Less than half of the 200 varieties are harmful to people. However, it's believed there may be as many as 200,000 species of jellies yet to be discovered.

In 1990 marine biologists first discovered the Immortal Jellyfish. Known as the Benjamin Button of the sea, this creature has the ability to age backwards. When it's threatened with environmental stress or physical assault, it transforms its mature self back into a polyp stage—and basically starts its life over again. Like an egg that hatches into a chicken that turns back into an egg an innumerable number of times, the pinto bean-sized Immortal Jellyfish is an incredible anomaly of the animal kingdom.

THE ILLUSION OF YOUTH

Unlike the Immortal Jellyfish, we age only one way—forward. No amount of exercise, antioxidants, anti-aging creams or plastic surgery can reverse that process. Unfortunately, our culture has tricked us into believing that "youth" is the best season of life. After that, it's all downhill... Or, is it?

Recent research has shown that for most adults getting older does indeed make us wiser. At the same time, it also makes us happier. As the years go by, we gain a broader, more balanced, perspective on what's important in life. We cast off the small stuff. We focus on what matters most. Sure, we may bemoan the fact that our bodies no longer look, or feel, like they did in our twenties. But we strive to discover the unique potential every changing season of our lives holds. Or, at least, we should.

Take time today to consider the benefits of your current stage in life. Focus on what you've gained over the years, instead of what you've lost. Your story is still being written. Don't waste a page trying to revise earlier chapters. Use the gift of each day to write something wholly new.

How many are your works, LORD! In wisdom
you made them all; the earth is full of your
creatures. There is the sea, vast and spacious,
teeming with creatures beyond number—
living things both large and small.
Psalm 104:24-25 NIV

EACH PART OF LIFE HAS ITS OWN PLEASURES.
EACH HAS ITS OWN ABUNDANT HARVEST,
TO BE GARNERED IN SEASON...OLD AGE IS THE
CONSUMMATION OF LIFE, RICH IN BLESSINGS.
CICERO

He hath made every thing beautiful in his time.
Ecclesiastes 3:11

TO BE INTERESTED IN THE CHANGING SEASONS
IS A HAPPIER STATE OF MIND
THAN TO BE HOPELESSLY IN LOVE WITH SPRING.
GEORGE SANTAYANA

I don't believe in ageing. I believe in forever
altering one's aspect to the sun.
Hence, my optimism.
Virginia Woolf

AGE SHOULD NOT HAVE ITS FACE LIFTED BUT IT
SHOULD RATHER TEACH THE WORLD TO ADMIRE
WRINKLES AS THE ETCHINGS OF EXPERIENCE AND
THE FIRM LINES OF CHARACTER.
RALPH BARTON PERRY

To every thing there is a season, and a time to
every purpose under the heaven.
Ecclesiastes 3:1

AS FOR OLD AGE, EMBRACE AND LOVE IT.
IT ABOUNDS WITH PLEASURE
IF YOU KNOW HOW TO USE IT.
SENECA

Humpbacks: Aquatic Artists

Humpback whales are like the performing arts majors of the sea. They're incredibly musical and acrobatic. The fact that adult males weigh 40 to 50 tons makes their tail lobbing, spyhopping, flipper slapping and twirling while breaching even more remarkable.

But, where humpbacks really excel is singing. Each of the humpbacks' three geographical groups has its own unique song. These complex compositions (sung only by males) combine moans, howls and cries into a tune that can be heard up to 20 miles away. Each song lasts 10 to 20 minutes, but is repeated for hours at a time.

But scientists aren't quite sure how. Whales don't have vocal chords. It's thought whales vocalize by forcing air through their circulatory system. Yet, no air escapes from their bodies and their mouths don't move. Scientists hypothesize whales sing and dance to communicate with each other or attract a mate, but they're not certain about that either. It's one of those fascinating animal facts only God knows for sure.

The Puzzle of Praise

Why do we dance and sing? The easy answer is: "Because it's fun." But if we're honest with ourselves, we know there's more going on behind the scenes. There's something that stirs up within us in response to music. And sometimes that music seems to be coming from deep inside. We hum in the shower. We sing along the trail. We feel a literal bounce in our step when life is going well.

Not everything in our lives—or in the animal kingdom—can be scientifically qualified, categorized or clarified. We hope when life seems hopeless. We love even when it costs us. We tear up at the sight of wild horses racing across an open field. We dance and sing and write and paint and play the saxophone. We worship.

Worship may sound like a very churchy word. But all it means is that we're expressing our love, joy and gratitude upward toward God. Sometimes we make a conscious effort to worship, to say "thanks." Sometimes, it simply flows from us in response to the amazing world our Creator has allowed us to live in. Who knows? Perhaps whales worship, too.

Ye shall go out with joy, and be led forth with peace: the mountains and hills shall break forth before you into singing, and all the trees of the fields shall clap their hands.

Isaiah 55:12

WORSHIP IS TRANSCENDENT WONDER.
THOMAS CARLYLE

Thou has turned for me
my mourning into dancing.
Psalm 30:11

TILL YOU CAN SING AND REJOICE AND DELIGHT
IN GOD, AS MISERS DO IN GOLD, AND KINGS IN
SCEPTERS, YOU NEVER ENJOY THE WORLD.
THOMAS TRAHERNE

Worship is the mind's humble
acquiescence to the fact of God.
Peter C. Moore

HE HATH PUT A NEW SONG IN MY MOUTH.
PSALM 40:3

Worship is the celebration of life in its totality.
William Stringfellow

THE WORSHIP OF GOD
IS NOT A RULE OF SAFETY —
IT IS AN ADVENTURE OF THE SPIRIT.
ALFRED NORTH WHITEHEAD

Oddly Adorable Armadillos

Armadillos look like some kind of holdover from the Pleistocene Era. Well, either that or a small armored car. In other words, they aren't very cuddly. But when it comes to being amazing, armadillos hold their own.

These reptiles have a quirky gift for being able to hold their breath for 6 minutes. So, when it comes to water they have two choices. They can walk along the bottom of a pond or ditch, because their hard, boney plates weigh them down. Or, they can swallow air, inflating their stomachs like a built-in life preserver, and swim across.

Unfortunately, armadillos don't do as well around roads as they do water. They're often hit by cars in Texas and surrounding states. Their problem isn't that they're slow to cross the road. It's just that armadillos jump straight up into the air 3 to 4 feet when they're startled. This often throws them right into the path of oncoming traffic. It's little wonder they've been nicknamed the Hillbilly Speed Bump.

PUTTING OFF THE INEVITABLE

Armadillos have another amazing talent. Though the gestation period for pregnant females is usually 4 to 5 months, they can delay giving birth for up to 2 1/2 years—if they feel so inclined. Talk about procrastination!

Obviously, humans lack this ability. We can't put off labor. But we would, if we could. When we feel overwhelmed by an impending task, our first inclination is often to move it down the To Do list. We put off making a confrontational call. We watch TV, instead of cleaning the garage. We sleep in, assuring ourselves we'll exercise...tomorrow.

Instead of relieving stress, procrastination adds to it. The longer we wait, the bigger the dreaded responsibility seems to grow. The best way to face the inevitable is to make a list of what you've been putting off. Then, each day (or once a week, if the projects are especially time consuming), do one thing on that list. As your list gets shorter, your load will feel lighter. Once it does, challenge yourself to change your ways. Do the tough stuff first. Then, instead of dreading the future, you can start looking forward to it.

O Lord, may I be directed what to do
and what to leave undone.
Elizabeth Fry

THE MAN WHO REMOVES A MOUNTAIN BEGINS
BY CARRYING AWAY SMALL STONES.
PROVERB

Nothing will be attempted if all possible
objections must first be overcome.
Samuel Johnson

EVEN IF YOU'RE ON THE RIGHT TRACK,
YOU'LL GET RUN OVER IF YOU JUST SIT THERE.
WILL ROGERS

God has promised forgiveness
to your repentance,
but He has not promised tomorrow
to your procrastination.
Augustine of Hippo

PUTTING OFF AN EASY THING
MAKES IT HARD.
PUTTING OFF A HARD THING
MAKES IT IMPOSSIBLE.
GEORGE CLAUDE LORIMER

Can anything be sadder than work unfinished?
Yes; work never begun.
Christina Rossetti

WHILE WE ARE POSTPONING, LIFE SPEEDS BY.
SENECA

A TURTLE'S RACE FOR SURVIVAL

Loggerheads have to win the turtle "lottery" just to survive their first minutes of life. They start off as ping pong ball-sized eggs, buried beneath the sand on the same beach where their mother was born. Sixty days later, just after sunset, the hatchlings head to the sea with their 30 to 100 siblings. (Their gender is determined by the temperature of the nest!)

The turtles follow the brightest light they see, which is usually the horizon of the ocean, the reflection of the moon on the water or phosphorescence in the waves. Unfortunately, artificial lights nearby can disorient them, leading them the wrong direction. Those who head the right direction still have to survive a gauntlet of crabs and sea birds looking for dinner. Once in the water, the young turtles need to escape being eaten by sharks.

Only one in one thousand loggerheads reaches adulthood. But if they make it that far, they can live 50 to 100 years.

How Are Your Odds?

If loggerhead turtles understood their odds of survival, they'd probably be pretty discouraged. They might even refuse to go to all the hard work of breaking out of their shell knowing the battle that lay ahead. They'd be so stressed over finding the "right" light they might stop dead in their tracks, afraid of making the wrong decision. Their fear and indecision would actually decrease their chances of survival. Aren't you glad we're not turtles?

We know all about odds. At times, we look at our circumstances and can't help but lament how we just can't catch a break. But what we know, and what we can see, doesn't tell the whole story. Only God knows that story from beginning to end.

When you feel dead in the water, faced with a difficult decision or simply too discouraged to want to make any decision at all, pray your way into God's presence. Ask for His guidance to help you know which way to turn, His strength to help you continue moving forward, and His peace to rest in His love, regardless of the stormy circumstances brewing around you, God is your rock, and refuge.

To do anything in this world worth doing, we
must not stand back shivering and thinking of
the cold and danger, but jump in and scramble
through as well as we can.
Sydney Smith

I CAN DO ALL THINGS THROUGH CHRIST
WHICH STRENGTHENETH ME.
PHILIPPIANS 4:13

If God be our God, He will give us peace
in trouble. When there is a storm without,
He will make peace within.
The world can create trouble in peace,
but God can create peace in trouble.
Thomas Watson

WITH GOD NOTHING SHALL BE IMPOSSIBLE.
LUKE 1:37

There is only one way to get ready for
immortality, and that is to love this life
and live it as bravely and faithfully
and cheerfully as we can.
Henry Van Dyke

IF GOD BE FOR US, WHO CAN BE AGAINST US?
ROMANS 8:31

Thanks be to God, which giveth us the victory
through our Lord Jesus Christ.
1 Corinthians 15:57

PEACE I LEAVE WITH YOU,
MY PEACE I GIVE UNTO YOU:
NOT AS THE WORLD GIVETH,
GIVE I UNTO YOU.
LET NOT YOUR HEART BE TROUBLED,
NEITHER LET IT BE AFRAID.
JOHN 14:27

Who Am I?

What runs as fast as a rabbit, cools itself by licking its arms, gives birth to babies the size of jellybeans and has a cry that sounds like a cross between a burp and a bellow? It's the koala bear. But the koala isn't a bear. It's a marsupial. Like its cousin the kangaroo, the koala sports a pouch which doubles as a nursery.

An Australian native, the word "koala" comes from the Aborigine word for "no water." That's because the koala gets most of the water it needs from its diet of eucalyptus leaves. There are over 600 varieties of eucalyptus trees, but each individual koala sticks to just two or three kinds. Being such picky eaters is one reason the koala population has dropped 90% in the last decade. Though koalas have recently been classified as "endangered," and are now protected by law, their food source is not. As eucalyptus forests become more scarce, so does the koala.

Running on Empty

Koalas munch on leaves when they're thirsty. We head for the nearest water fountain. But what happens when we're spiritually thirsty? Do we even recognize how parched we are?

We all occassionally try to go too hard and do too much on too little spiritual nourishment. Then we get busy, distracted, selfish and controlling. We attempt to carry the problems of the world on our own feeble shoulders. When we're feeling anxious, irritable or have an overall dissatisfaction with life, it's good to remember that these may be signs of spiritual dehydration. In the same way that feeling the discomfort of thirst encourages us to drink water, feeling an unease about life leads us back to what our soul naturally craves.

Quench your spiritual thirst with some quiet time. Read a few Psalms. Talk to God. Take a walk and enjoy His art gallery of nature. Drink in the pleasure of God's presence wherever you are. He's always near, ready to refill you with hope, joy and peace.

O God, thou art my God; early will I seek thee:
my soul thirsteth for thee,
my flesh longeth for thee in a
dry and thirsty land, where no water is.
Psalm 63:1

My spirit has become dry
because it forgets to feed on you.
John of the Cross

O taste and see that the Lord is good.
Psalm 34:8

O God, I have tasted thy goodness,
and it has both satisfied me
and made me thirsty for more.
A.W. Tozer

Thou hast made us for Thyself, and the heart of
man is restless until it finds rest in Thee.
Augustine of Hippo

Man doth not live by bread alone, but by
every word that proceedeth
out of the mouth of the Lord.
Deuteronomy 8:3

Hard as the world is to explain with God, it is
harder yet without Him.
Claude G. Montefiore

Every creature is a divine word
because it proclaims God.
Bonaventure

THE MONARCH'S MYSTERIOUS MIGRATION

There are 15,000 to 20,000 species of butterfly. But there's only one that migrates 2,500 miles to a predesignated hibernation spot. Yet only 25% of all monarchs are lucky enough to make the journey. Every year, four generations of monarchs are born. The first three die less than six weeks after emerging from their cocoons. But the fourth generation lives six to eight months—long enough for them to fly to Mexico or southern California for the winter. Year after year the next "fourth generation" of monarchs returns to the same spot, resting in the same trees along their migratory route.

Like birds, monarch use thermals (warm updrafts of air) to help move them forward on their journey, while helping them conserve energy. It's believed they also rely on the sun and on the earth's magnetic field to guide them to their winter home. But no one can really explain how that perfect snowbird spot is hard-wired so perfectly into their DNA.

Headed Home

Monarchs aren't the only ones who instinctively know the way home—even when "home" is a place they've never been before. We've been given that same gift. We're hard-wired for heaven. We long for it off and on during our lifetime, for that place where we can rest, where peace abounds, where hate, violence and fear is a distant memory. A place where there's no such thing as a broken heart. A place where everything feels "right."

The Bible only gives us a glimpse of what lies beyond this life. Perhaps that's the way it needs to be. After all, we're not there yet. We have a life that's meant to be lived to the fullest right here and now. But just like the monarchs, when the time is right, we will make the journey home. We don't need to cross our fingers, hoping we're one of the lucky "fourth generation." God's promised that eternal life is a reality for each of us who chooses to draw close to Him. His love is our homing beacon. It cannot fail to lead us to the place our hearts long to go.

Eye hath not seen, nor ear heard, neither have
entered into the heart of man,
the things which God hath prepared
for them that love him.
1 Corinthians 2:9

THE ONLY AIR OF THE SOUL, IN WHICH IT CAN
BREATHE AND LIVE, IS THE PRESENT GOD AND
THE SPIRITS OF THE JUST: THAT IS OUR HEAVEN,
OUR HOME, OUR ALL-RIGHT PLACE.
GEORGE MACDONALD

Life is the childhood of our immortality.
Johann von Goethe

IF THERE WERE NO FUTURE LIFE,
OUR SOULS WOULD NOT THIRST FOR IT.
JEAN PAUL RICHTER

I have never seen what to me seemed an atom of
proof that there is a future life...
And yet—I am strongly inclined to expect one.
Mark Twain

OUR CREATOR WOULD NEVER HAVE MADE SUCH
LOVELY DAYS, AND HAVE GIVEN US THE DEEP
HEARTS TO ENJOY THEM, ABOVE AND BEYOND
ALL THOUGHT, UNLESS WE WERE MEANT TO BE
IMMORTAL.
NATHANIEL HAWTHORNE

Our Father which art in heaven,
Hallowed be thy name. Thy kingdom come...
Matthew 6:9-10

LIFE'S A VOYAGE THAT'S HOMEWARD BOUND.
HERMAN MELVILLE

ALL THINGS BRIGHT AND BEAUTIFUL

BY CECIL FRANCES ALEXANDER

All things bright and beautiful,
All things great and small,
All things wise and wonderful,
The Lord God made them all.

Each little flower that opens,
Each little bird that sings,
He made their glowing colors,
He made their tiny wings.

The purple-headed mountain,
  The river running by,
The sunset, and the morning,
  That brightens up the sky;

The cold wind in the winter,
  The pleasant summer sun,
The ripe fruits in the garden,
  He made them every one.

He gave us eyes to see them,
  And lips that we might tell,
How great is God Almighty,
Who has made all things well.

THE MORE I STUDY NATURE,
THE MORE I STAND AMAZED
AT THE WORK OF THE CREATOR.

LOUIS PASTEUR